MY FIRST BOOK OF
DINOSAUR
COMPARISONS

Brimming with creative inspiration, how-to projects, and useful information to enrich your everyday life, Quarto Knows is a favorite destination for those pursuing their interests and passions. Visit our site and dig deeper with our books into your area of interest: Quarto Creates, Quarto Cooks, Quarto Homes, Quarto Lives, Quarto Drives, Quarto Explores, Quarto Gifts, or Quarto Kids.

© 2021 Quarto Publishing plc

First published in 2021 by Happy Yak,
an imprint of The Quarto Group.
26391 Crown Valley Parkway, Suite 220,
Mission Viejo, CA 92691, USA
T: +1 949 380 7510
F: +1 949 380 7575
www.quartoknows.com

Designer: Kate Haynes
Editor: Hannah Dove
Fact-checker: Barbara Taylor
Creative Director: Malena Stojic
Associate Publisher: Rhiannon Findlay

ISBN 978-0-7112-6075-7

Manufactured in Guangdong, China TT042021

1 3 5 7 9 10 8 6 4 2

MIX
Paper from responsible sources
FSC® C016973

MY FIRST BOOK OF
DINOSAUR
COMPARISONS

WRITTEN BY SARA HURST
ILLUSTRATED BY ANA SEIXAS

happy yak

CONTENTS

ABOUT THIS BOOK

Did you know that Apatosaurus could whip its tail faster than the speed of sound? Or that Argentinosaurus was as heavy as 12 African bush elephants? OR that T. rex could crush a car in a single bite? These are called comparisons.

A comparison isn't just a fun way to describe something—it is useful, too. This is because noticing what is different or the same about two things is a great way to learn about them.

This exciting book is PACKED with comparisons all about dinosaurs, as well as some of the other prehistoric animals and plants they shared the planet with. You can compare details like heights, weights, speeds, time periods, defense tactics, fossil types, diets, feathers, and more.

And that's not all—there's a guide to saying the animals' names and there are fun challenges and quizzes to tackle, too!

SAY THE NAME

First, find out how to pronounce the names of the dinosaurs and other prehistoric animals you will meet in the book.

ALLOSAURUS
AL-oh-SORE-us

AMARGASAURUS
a-marg-ah-SORE-us

ANCHIORNIS
ANG-kee-OR-niss

ANKYLOSAURUS
ANG-kee-low-SORE-us

ANUROGNATHUS
an-YOO-rog-NAY-thus

APATOSAURUS
a-PAT-oh-SORE-us

ARCHAEOPTERYX
AR-kee-OP-ter-ix

ARCHELON
ARK-eh-lon

ARGENTINOSAURUS
ar-gen-TEEN-oh-SORE-us

BARYONYX
ba-ree-ON-ix

BRACHIOSAURUS
BRAK-ee-oh-SORE-us

CARCHARODONTOSAURUS
kar-ka-ro-DON-toe-SORE-us

CAUDIPTERYX
caw-DIP-ter-ix

COMPSOGNATHUS
komp-SOG-nay-thus

DEINONYCHUS
die-NON-i-kus

DEINOSUCHUS
die-no-SOO-kus

DIPLODOCUS
dip-LOW-dock-us

DROMICEIOMIMUS
dro-MI-see-oh-MIME-us

EORAPTOR
EE-oh-RAP-tor

FRUITADENS
FROO-tah-denz

GALLIMIMUS
GAL-ee-MIME-us

GIGANOTOSAURUS
ji-GAN-oh-toe-SORE-us

HATZEGOPTERYX
HAT-zeg-OP-ter-ix

HYBODUS
hi-BO-dus

HYPSILOPHODON
HIP-sil-oh-FOE-don

LYSTROSAURUS
lie-stro-SORE-us

MAGNAPAULIA
MAG-na-PORE-lee-ah

MICRORAPTOR
MIKE-row-RAP-tor

MORGANUCODON
more-GAN-oo-ko-don

OVIRAPTOR
oh-VEE-rap-tor

PARASAUROLOPHUS
pa-ra-SORE-oh-LOAF-us

PATAGOTITAN
pat-ag-oh-TIE-ton

PLACERIAS
pla-SER-ree-us

PROSALIRUS
PRO-sa-lee-rus

PROTOCERATOPS
PRO-toe-SERRA-tops

PSITTACOSAURUS
SIT-a-koh-SORE-us

PTERANODON
teh-RAN-oh-don

PTERODACTYLUS
teh-ro-DAC-ti-lus

SAUROPOSEIDON
SORE-oh-po-SIDE-on

SHONISAURUS
show-nee-SORE-us

SORDES
SORE-dees

SPINOSAURUS
SPINE-oh-SORE-us

THERIZINOSAURUS
THER-ee-zine-oh-SORE-us

TRICERATOPS
tri-SERRA-tops

TYLOSAURUS
tie-low-SORE-us

TYRANNOSAURUS REX
tie-RAN-oh-SORE-us Rex

VEGAVIS
VEY-gah-vis

VELOCIRAPTOR
vel-OSS-ee-RAP-tor

YUTYRANNUS
YOO-tie-RAN-us

BACK IN TIME

Dinosaurs lived an incredibly lo-o-o-ng time ago in three massive blocks of time, called the Triassic, Jurassic, and Cretaceous periods. Let's compare the differences in each time period.

TRIASSIC PERIOD: 252–200 MYA

During this time, all of Earth's land was joined together in one giant continent, called Pangaea.

EORAPTOR

The first dinosaurs appeared and lived in this period, including Eoraptor, a tiny predator who would have been SHORTER than you are.

JURASSIC PERIOD: 200–145 MYA

In this period, the Earth's land broke apart to make several huge land masses, divided by the oceans.

The temperatures were slightly COOLER, and more rain fell.

SEQUOIA

Plants and trees flourished. The land was covered with lush ferns as well as tall forests of sequoia trees.

CRETACEOUS PERIOD: 145–66 MYA

During this period, the Earth's land masses split up even more and moved FARTHER apart.

BARYONYX

Fierce meat-eating dinosaurs ruled the land, including Baryonyx who snacked on fish and other marine creatures.

CYCAD

GINKGO

FERN

Other animals, including fish and turtles, lived in this period, too.

The land was covered with deserts and the climate was hot and dry.

The plants that covered the land were mostly ferns, ginkgos, and cycads.

Toward the end of this period, there were lots of earthquakes and volcanic eruptions.

DIPLODOCUS   **ALLOSAURUS**

ARCHAEOPTERYX

Massive plant-eating dinosaurs feasted on the plants while terrifying meat-eating dinosaurs feasted on them!

Archaeopteryx lived in this period. This flying dinosaur was an ancestor of modern birds.

At the end of the Cretaceous period, the dinosaurs died out. Scientists think an asteroid that hit the Earth may have changed the climate so fast that the dinosaurs could not survive.

MAGNOLIA

Butterflies, bees, and snakes lived on the land.

The first flowering plants appeared.

FOSSIL CLUES

We learn about dinosaurs by studying fossils, the remains that were left after they died. Let's find out about four fossil types.

Sue's massive skull was about as LONG as a 10-year-old child!

BONES
Bones are the most common fossils. They tell us a lot, from how big dinosaurs were to how they walked. One famous T. rex fossil skeleton was found in the US. It was named "Sue" after the person who first spotted it.

AMBER
Sometimes parts of dinosaurs got trapped in sticky tree resin, which hardened into amber fossils. These fossils are super special because they can include skin and feathers.

Scientists found a tiny part of a dinosaur's feathery tail in an amber fossil. It was SHORTER than your little finger! The full tail may have been much longer.

POOP!
We can learn a lot from rare fossil poop. For example, poop full of crunched-up bones tells us the dinosaur who left it was a meat-eater with strong, sharp teeth.

One of the biggest fossil poops ever found was almost 30 inches long and HEAVIER than a bowling ball!

Some of the tiniest dino tracks found so far were found in South Korea. Scientists think the prints may have been made by a teeny dinosaur the size of a sparrow.

TRACKS
Did you know that footprints can be fossilized too? Footprints can reveal a lot, including the length, weight, and speed of the dinosaur who left the tracks.

FROM EGG TO ADULT

Dinosaurs grew bigger than any other land animal, but how fast did they grow? See how much time it took for a T. rex to change from a cute baby into a fearsome adult!

EGG
Like all known dinosaurs, T. rex started life as an egg. No one knows how big a T. rex egg was or what it looked like because none have been found yet. What do you think they were like?

BABY
A hatchling was about as BIG as a small turkey. It looked teeny-tiny compared to its parents! It had a soft, fluffy feather covering like a modern baby chick.

It already had sharp teeth.

JUVENILE
By age 10 a young T. rex was about as HEAVY as a male polar bear. It still had its baby teeth, which were like sharp, thin blades.

EGG SIZE
Dinosaur eggs were usually round or oval. Some looked like a long potato! The biggest eggs today are ostrich eggs. The biggest dinosaur eggs we know of were three times BIGGER than an ostrich egg, and shaped like a giant football.

When a T. rex's teeth wore out, they grew new ones. Sharks and crocodiles can do this today.

TEEN

Whoosh! Like humans, a T. rex grew and changed fastest in its teenage years. By age 15 it was TALLER than an adult man. And there was still more growing to do!

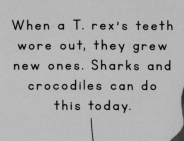

ADULT

By age 20 a T. rex was fully grown. It was twice as LONG as teenage T. rex and about as HEAVY as four family cars! Its teeth were massive bone-crunching weapons.

GROWTH RINGS

To figure out a dinosaur's age when it died, scientists count growth rings. These are circles inside dinosaur bones. If a dinosaur was 25 when it died, it would have 25 growth rings inside its bones.

LIVING TOGETHER

Dinosaurs didn't live lonely lives. Some came together to live, nest, or hunt in groups. Compare how different dinosaurs cooperated, then see if you can match them to similar modern-day animals.

HERDS

Living in a group helped many plant-eating dinosaurs to survive.

APATOSAURUS

An Apatosaurus was HEAVIER than a fire truck, but a large meat-eater or a pack of predators could still take one down. Living in a herd made it much harder for enemies to attack these giant dinosaurs.

HYPSILOPHODON

These small dinosaurs relied on each other to look out for danger, then used their speed to dash away and escape hungry predators.

NESTS

Some dinosaurs nested together in huge groups. This way, there were plenty of adults to keep watch and defend the eggs and babies.

OVIRAPTOR

Oviraptor moms nested together. Each mom would lay between 5 and 20 eggs in a round, open nest and lie on top of them to keep them warm and safe.

PACKS

Some meat-eating dinosaurs hunted as a team, working together to pick off massive plant-eaters.

DEINONYCHUS

These cunning dinosaurs were about as TALL as a 13-year-old child. They worked in packs to bring down prey much larger than themselves.

QUICK QUIZ

Each modern animal below acts in a similar way as one of the dinosaurs on the page. Can you match them up?

Turn to page 48 to check your answers.

WOLF

GAZELLE

PENGUIN

ELEPHANT

PREHISTORIC PLANTS

Did you know that some of the plants, trees, and flowers that covered the land when the dinosaurs lived are still around today? Take a look ...

FERNS

These plants have been around since BEFORE the dinosaurs and still grow around the world today.

A tree fern can grow about as TALL as two giraffes.

MAGNOLIA TREES

Flowering plants, such as magnolias, first grew in the Cretaceous period. They spread quickly all over the Earth and still bloom today. Their leaves, flowers, fruit, and seeds made good food for dinosaurs.

One magnolia flower can grow as BIG as a dinner plate!

CYCADS

Cycads thrived during the time of the dinosaurs. Some types still grow today, but there are far fewer of them.

One cycad seed can be as HEAVY as about four bowling balls!

X4

GINKGOS

Ginkgos are some of the oldest trees we know of. They appeared around the same time as the first dinosaurs. Only one species, or type of ginkgo tree, is alive today. Scientists call it a "living fossil" because it hasn't really changed in 200 million years.

In fall, the unusual fan-shaped leaves turn bright yellow and drop from the branches.

A ginkgo tree trunk is about as WIDE as two children standing fingertip to fingertip.

SEQUOIAS

Vast forests of these towering trees appeared in the Jurassic period. Today, they only grow in North America.

These gigantic trees can reach heights as TALL as a 26-floor building!

Sequoias were one of the main food sources for the massive plant-eating dinosaurs, including Brachiosaurus.

SUPER-SIZE

Say hi to some GIGANTIC dinosaurs! See how they size up next to buildings, to vehicles, and to us humans.

ARGENTINOSAURUS

The longest-ever dinosaur was as LONG as about four fire trucks and as HEAVY as about six fire trucks. It was so hefty that the ground would shake when it walked. But there's no need to be scared of this gentle giant—it only ate plants.

TRICERATOPS

The smallest dinosaur in the picture is still impressive. It was as LONG and as TALL as a bulldozer. Its size and shape were similar to an African bush elephant's and its horns make you think of a rhino.

SAUROPOSEIDON

This enormous dinosaur was as TALL as a six-floor building! When it was hungry it stre-e-e-tched its superlong neck to nibble on the topmost tree leaves.

BRACHIOSAURUS

This plant-eating dinosaur was SMALLER than Sauroposeidon but still pretty huge! It was as TALL as a four-floor building. Its name means "arm lizard." It got this name because its front legs were longer than its back legs, so they look like arms!

TYRANNOSAURUS REX

This fierce meat-eater was LONGER than a London bus and tall enough to peek in the top windows! It hunted other dinosaurs, crunching them up with 60 pointed teeth. That's more than twice as many teeth as you have.

PET-SIZE

How cute! These dinosaurs were small enough to keep as house pets. See how they compare to some familiar animal friends. Which dino pet would you choose?

MICRORAPTOR

This teeny dinosaur was about twice as LONG as a cockatoo. It walked on two legs and looked a lot like a bird. Its four wings helped it to glide through the air.

CLUE: *Microraptor ate only meat. It hunted all kinds of small animals.*

PROTOCERATOPS

Protoceratops was a bit of a mixed-up creature. It had a beak like a parrot's and scaly skin like a lizard. It was about the same size as a miniature horse.

CLUE: *Protoceratops's sharp beak was good for snipping off tough, tasty leaves.*

FRUITADENS

This funny-looking dinosaur was LIGHTER than a guinea pig! Fruitadens was so light because the bones in its back legs were hollow. Its tail was two times LONGER than its head and body put together.

CLUE: *Fruitadens liked to eat a mix of meat and plant foods.*

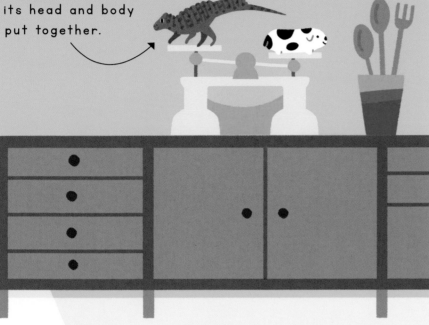

COMPSOGNATHUS

This nimble dinosaur was as TALL as a poodle and built to chase things! Its light, narrow body and long tail helped it to run fast without losing its balance.

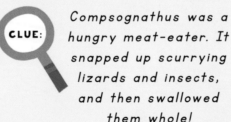

CLUE: *Compsognathus was a hungry meat-eater. It snapped up scurrying lizards and insects, and then swallowed them whole!*

QUICK QUIZ

It's dinnertime! Look for the clues near each dinosaur then match the food to its owner.

Turn to page 48 to check your answers.

1.

2.

3.

4.

23

DINOSAUR WEIGH-IN

Feast your eyes on these four dinosaurs. You wouldn't want one of them to step or sit on you! Find out which was the heaviest and see how they compare to one of today's heftiest animals.

ANKYLOSAURUS

The lightest dinosaur on the page was as HEAVY as one African bush elephant.

Can you see the bony bumps and spikes all over it? They acted like armor to protect it when bigger dinosaurs attacked.

Patagotitan's thick, strong legs carried its huge weight. It was too heavy to walk or run very fast.

PATAGOTITAN

This massive heavyweight was as HEAVY as 12 African bush elephants.

AFRICAN BUSH ELEPHANT

These elephants are the heaviest land animals alive today. One African bush elephant is HEAVIER than three cars!

MAGNAPAULIA

This strange looking dinosaur lived in wetlands and may have been a swimmer. It was about as HEAVY as four African bush elephants.

Magnapaulia was three times LIGHTER than Patagotitan.

GIGANOTOSAURUS

Watch out! This ferocious hunter had jagged teeth and was a similar type of dinosaur to T. rex, only bigger and heavier.

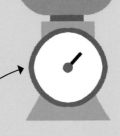

Giganotosaurus weighed about the same as two African bush elephants.

DINOSAUR DINNERS

All dinosaurs got their energy from food, just like you do. Let's see what was on the menu and compare different dinosaur dinners.

The bigger piece of this pie chart shows that about two-thirds of dinosaurs were herbivores (plant-eaters).

The smaller piece shows that about one-third of dinosaurs were carnivores (meat-eaters) or omnivores (plant and meat eaters).

THE VEGGIE SUPREME

Diplodocus was a sauropod (a large, long-necked, four-legged, plant-eating dinosaur) and it was LONGER than a tennis court! In order to keep its massive body moving, Diplodocus had to eat A LOT. It ate nonstop, gulping down plants for breakfast, lunch, and dinner. Its blunt, peglike teeth were perfect for pulling leaves from branches.

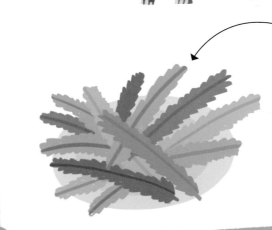

Diplodocus had to munch through about 73 lbs of ferns every day. That's the same as you eating 66 boxes of cereal every day!

THE MEAT FEASTER

The most famous meat-eating dinosaur is probably T. rex. It was both a hunter and a scavenger who wolfed down the leftovers of other predators. It had sawlike teeth and its jaws could crush bones!

Scientists think T. rex ate like big meat-eaters today, such as lions who eat a lot at once and then might go some time before their next meal.

T. rex would eat smaller, plant-eating dinosaurs such as Triceratops, especially when they were young or weak.

THE UNFUSSY EATER

Scientists think Gallimimus may have mixed up its meals—snacking on both meat and plants. It had a toothless beak and swallowed its food whole! Comblike ridges in its mouth may have helped Gallimimus filter food from muddy water, like ducks do today. Its clawlike fingers also helped it to root through soil to find food.

Gallimimus may have snacked on small animals, insects, seeds, eggs, and plants.

EXPERT HUNTERS

Many meat-eating dinosaurs were smart, powerful, and armed with deadly weapons! See how these two fearsome attackers compare to each other, and to hunters today.

VELOCIRAPTOR

Though it was only as TALL as a turkey, this dinosaur was a mean killing machine! It hunted all types of smaller creatures, including baby dinosaurs. Velociraptor is famous for its speed. It could run twice as FAST as a T. rex.

It couldn't fly, but its feathered wings may have helped its speedy moves.

Razor-sharp teeth tore mea from its prey.

Modern birds of prey, such as eagles, grab and trap their prey in a similar way.

Velociraptor's strong claws were deadly weapons. It used the bigger curved claws o each back foot to sta and hook its victims s they couldn't escape!

CARCHARODONTOSAURUS

This deadly hunter's name means "shark tooth lizard." It got this name because each of its 8-inch-long teeth was razor sharp and jagged, like those of a great white shark.

Modern wolves use their sharp senses to track their prey like Carcharodontosaurus.

This dinosaur used its senses to hunt its prey. Its sharp hearing picked up sounds, its nose sniffed out other animals, and its eyes spotted movement.

Its huge mouth was filled with more than 60 terrifying teeth.

Carcharodontosaurus's head was as BIG as a bathtub, and its jaws and neck were strong enough to pick up animals HEAVIER than a grizzly bear!

QUICK QUIZ

Carcharodontosaurus's eyes faced OUT from the sides of its head. T. rex's eyes faced FORWARD. Can you guess whose eyesight was better?

Turn to page 48 to check your answer.

Its three-clawed fingers were good for gripping struggling prey. Yikes!

DEADLY DEFENDERS

Plant-eating dinosaurs had different ways of protecting themselves from attackers. Find out how their defenses compare to each other, and to modern animals.

ANKYLOSAURUS
This dinosaur was as TALL as a man and as HEAVY as an African bush elephant. It was built a bit like a tank. Bony armor covered most of its body, and it carried a serious weapon—its tail!

Bony spikes protected Ankylosaurus's back and sides, and big bite-proof plates protected the neck and shoulders

Modern crocodiles have similar tough, knobbly skin to Ankylosaurus.

With a heavy, bony club on the end of its tail, Ankylosaurus could land a killer blow with one swish.

Its soft underbelly wasn't protected, but a super heavy dinosaur was hard to flip over!

The solid skull acted like a crash helmet. Even the eyelids were armor-plated.

30

Modern rhinos usually have one or two horns on their faces. Like Triceratops, they use their horns to defend themselves.

TRICERATOPS

This dinosaur may look slow because of its big, bulky body, but you wouldn't want to get too close. It was surprisingly speedy and could charge at enemies two times FASTER than a modern elephant!

The neck frill stuck up like a bony shield. It had hard points around it for even more protection.

Its skin was tough and scaly. An attacker's teeth would need to be extra sharp and strong to bite through it.

This dinosaur was as HEAVY as two African bush elephants. Its size would have made it harder to attack.

The three horns on Triceratops's face were its best weapons. The longer horns were sharp enough to wound predators such as T. rex, and could each grow up to 3 feet—that's as LONG as a golf club!

AWESOME ABILITIES

Different dinosaurs had different skills to help them survive and thrive. Let's find out about some of these awesome abilities.

SUPERSONIC SWING

Apatosaurus was a sauropod dinosaur. Like all sauropods, Apatosaurus had a super-long tail, and some scientists believe it could swing it side-to-side at astonishing speeds.

It may have whipped its tail to swat away nasty predators. Ouch!

The speed of the tail would create a shockwave and make a sonic boom—a loud cracking noise.

Apatosaurus could whip its tail up to three times FASTER than the world's fastest train! In fact, scientists think Apatosaurus could move its tail at supersonic speed (faster than the speed of sound).

'SPEEDY SPRINT

Some dinosaurs were much speedier than others and Dromiceiomimus might have been the speediest of all. It belonged to a group called the "ostrich mimic" dinosaurs and it even looked a bit like an ostrich!

Dromiceiomimus could run about as FAST as a modern ostrich and almost twice as fast as the FASTEST human sprinter.

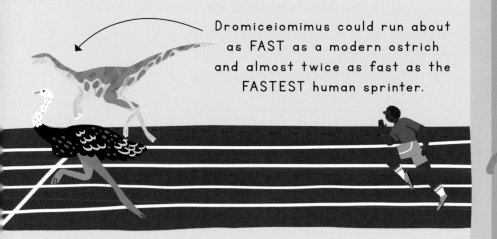

DEADLY POUNCE

Deinonychus—a fierce little meat-eater—would leap up high to land on top of its prey, much like a pouncing lion.

LION

DEINONYCHUS

BRUTAL BITE

T. rex had the most powerful bite of all the dinosaurs. In fact, scientists think it had the STRONGEST bite force of any land animal that has ever existed.

One human bite is only powerful enough to crush about six carrots!

One T. rex bite was powerful enough to crush a family car!

GLORIOUS GLIDE

Little Microraptor used its wings to glide from spot to spot, a bit like a modern flying squirrel.

FLYING SQUIRREL

MICRORAPTOR

SKY LIFE

When dinosaurs looked up, they saw pterosaurs soaring through the sky. Some of these flying reptiles were tiny, while others were GIGANTIC. Compare them to the creatures and machines that fill our skies today.

SORDES

Tiny Sordes was like a strange, hairy bird. Its wingspan was more than twice as WIDE as the wingspan of a little brown bat.

Its stiff tail was longer than its body and helped Sordes to fly straight.

PTERANODON

This awesome pterosaur's wingspan was very impressive. It was twice as WIDE as that of an albatross, which has the LONGEST wingspan of today's birds.

The long toothless beak was like a pelican's beak. Pteranodon used it to scoop fish from the waves.

PTERODACTYLUS

This pterosaur is a celebrity. It was the first one anyone studied. Before scientists realized that it was a reptile, they thought it could be a prehistoric bird, a bat, or even a sea creature. Its wingspan was about as WIDE as the wingspan of a seagull.

Its long jaws had 90 pointed teeth—more than three times as many as you!

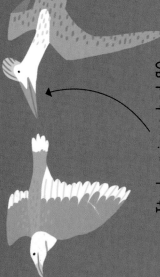

HATZEGOPTERYX

This ginormous pterosaur looked like a creature from space! When it stood up, Hatzegopteryx was as TALL as a giraffe and its wingspan was about as WIDE as a large hang glider.

It hunted land animals from above, including dinosaurs. Its beak and jaw opened wide enough to swallow prey whole ... Snap!

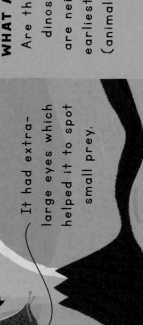

ANUROGNATHUS

Little Anurognathus was one of the first pterosaurs. It was only 4 inches long from nose to tail. That's about as LONG as a medium-size hummingbird.

It had extra-large eyes which helped it to spot small prey.

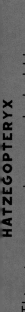

WHAT ARE PTEROSAURS?

Are they birds? Are they dinosaurs? Pterosaurs are neither! They are the earliest flying vertebrates (animals with a backbone).

ON THE GROUND

The dinosaurs may have been the stars of their time, but they shared their world with lots of other land animals. Some were huge reptiles and others were teeny mammals. Take a look!

PLACERIAS

This bulky beast of a reptile probably moved easier in water than on land. It was as HEAVY as a small car and about as LONG as a small hippo.

It had two tusks and a strong beak like a turtle's for slicing up its favorite food—tough, chewy plants.

MORGANUCODON

Most mammals living alongside the dinosaurs were small. This mini, mouselike creature was SMALL enough to fit in your hand, and weighed LESS than an apple!

PROSALIRUS

This teeny amphibian lived in the Jurassic period. Scientists think it could have been the first ever jumping frog. It was only 2 inches long—about as LONG as a large strawberry!

DEINOSUCHUS

This gigantic reptile was always hungry! It hunted on land and in water, and even attacked huge dinosaurs. It was as LONG as three American alligators, the biggest of all modern alligators.

The name Deinosuchus means "terrible crocodile."

LYSTROSAURUS

This odd-looking reptile was about as LONG and TALL as a modern pig. Like a pig, it loved mud! In fact, it spent much of its time digging.

Lystrosaurus pulled up tasty roots and plants with its two short tusks.

OCEAN LIFE

Huge marine reptiles lived in the oceans when the dinosaurs were alive. How would you like to swim with these amazing animals?

TYLOSAURUS
This enormous predator had a body like a giant lizard, and a long, powerful tail to help it swim fast. It was as LONG as three modern saltwater crocodiles.

Tylosaurus opened its jaws extra wide like a snake. It swallowed turtles, fish, and smaller reptiles in one huge gulp!

HYBODUS
This big fish was an early type of shark. It was LONGER than an adult man, but about two times SHORTER than a modern tiger shark.

Hybodus had sharp teeth at the front of its strong jaws for grabbing slippery fish, and flat back teeth for crushing shellfish.

SHONISAURUS

This reptile looked more like a big fish! It would come up to the surface to breathe air, then dive down deep to hunt for tasty fish and squid.

It had a long snout and four narrow flippers.

QUICK QUIZ

How many divers would it take to reach the length of Shonisaurus?

Turn to page 48 to check your answer.

ARCHELON

Meet Archelon, the ancestor of all sea turtles. It was two times BIGGER than the largest sea turtle alive today, the Leatherback.

THE OLDIES

Many animals that swim in our oceans today have been around since way BEFORE the dinosaurs. These animals include types of starfish, octopus, and jellyfish.

HUGE AND HUNGRY

Take a tour around this colossal plant-eater! Argentinosaurus was one of the largest of all the dinosaurs. Let's size up some of its features.

Argentinosaurus was huge, but its head—and brain—were tiny!

Its neck was about twice as LONG as its body.

This dinosaur ate without stopping. Its blunt teeth worked like fast tools; pulling leaves from trees before Argentinosaurus swallowed them whole.

You could easily run underneath this dinosaur! Its chunky legs were about twice as TALL as you.

From nose to tail this giant was about as LONG as six reticulated pythons.

HEAVYWEIGHT

Argentinosaurus was as HEAVY as about six fire trucks, or 12 African bush elephants. What a whopper!

X12

DEEP PRINTS

Argentinosaurus's footprints could sink more than 6 feet into the ground. That's DEEP enough for an adult to hide inside!

Ten huge back bones formed this part of the spine. Each was as BIG as a person!

Scientists think it may have been as TALL as a tower of about five adults.

Its tail was up to three times as LONG as its body.

This was one super pooper. The amount of poop it could produce in a day might have been as HEAVY as a small car!

41

FEATHERY FEATURES

Dinosaurs had scaly skin like modern lizards and crocodiles, but many grew feathers, too. Compare some famous fluffy dinosaurs.

YUTYRANNUS

This huge dinosaur was almost as LONG as a fire truck, and is the BIGGEST feathered dinosaur found so far. It had a long, shaggy coat of bristle feathers, like those of a modern emu. It lived in chilly forests, so scientists think the bristle feathers helped to keep it warm.

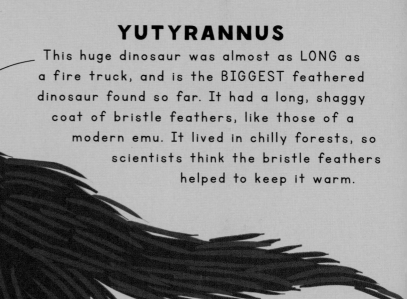

Each bristle feather on Yutyrannus was about as LONG as a pencil.

FEATHER TYPES

Dinosaurs had three kinds of feathers:

BRISTLE
Tubelike bristles, a bit like hair.

BRANCHED
Fanned out from a stiff stem, similar to the feathers of modern birds.

DOWN
Soft and fluffy, like the fuzz on a baby chick.

CAUDIPTERYX

Birdlike Caudipteryx had two types of feathers: fluffy down feathers on its body and branched feathers on its arms and tail. This dinosaur was about as BIG as a peacock and may have used its tail feathers like peacocks do—to attract mates.

Its branched tail feathers were about 8 inches long—that's as LONG as a large banana.

It couldn't fly, but may have used its short, feathered arms to help it steer as it ran.

ANCHIORNIS

This super feathery dinosaur was small enough to fit on these pages! Soft bristle and down feathers covered its body and tail. It couldn't fly, but stiff branched feathers on its arms and legs helped it to glide. The bright orange head feathers may have helped Anchiornis attract mates.

This tape measure shows you Anchiornis's length from beak to tail.

WEIRD AND WACKY

Have you noticed that certain dinosaurs had some seriously strange features? Take a look at just a few!

SPINY SAIL

This dragonlike dinosaur was called Spinosaurus, and it was the BIGGEST of all the meat-eating dinosaurs. Scientists think the strange, spiny sail along its back might have helped it to control its body heat.

PARROT FACE

This dinosaur is called Psittacosaurus, which means "parrot lizard." It was named this because its head and mouth were shaped like those of a parrot.

The bony spikes holding the sail up were huge. Each one was as TALL as a man.

Psittacosaurus walked on four legs. At over 6 feet long, it was at least twice as LONG as a macaw parrot.

SPIKY MANE

The double row of spines along Amargasaurus's back looked like a spiky horse's mane. The sharp spines pointed backward and may have been used to stab attackers.

The longest spikes were about as LONG as a man's arm.

SCISSOR HANDS

Therizinosaurus was a very odd-looking dinosaur. It had a tiny head, a huge belly, and three giant scissorlike claws on each hand. It had the LONGEST claws of any dinosaur or animal in Earth's history!

Each claw was nearly as LONG as a five-year-old child.

NOISY HEAD GEAR

Parasaurolophus had a strange head crest, made of long, hollow bones. Lots of dinosaurs had these crests. Scientists think they used them to make trumpetlike calls to each other.

STUBBY ARMS

T. rex had tiny arms compared to the rest of its body. Scientists are still working out why. What is your idea?

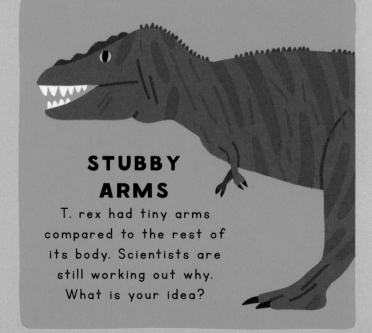

CRRRAAASH!

Scientists think the dinosaurs died out after a massive asteroid (a rock from space) smashed into Earth 66 million years ago. Let's find out more about this deadly disaster.

EARTH BEFORE

The Earth was warm and sunny. Plants covered the land, and a variety of land, air, and ocean animals thrived.

EARTH AFTER

The disaster destroyed much of the planet's animal and plant life, including the unlucky dinosaurs!

The world was cold and dark. Gigantic waves washed over the oceans and volcanoes erupted. The eruptions caused dust clouds, which blocked out sunlight.

The asteroid that hit Earth was huge. It was up to 9 miles WIDE—that's more than five times as LONG as the Golden Gate Bridge in San Francisco.

When it hit, the asteroid left a colossal crater in the Earth. It was so DEEP that the world's tallest mountain, Everest—with another Everest on top—could fit easily inside!

SURVIVORS

Most survivors were small meat-eaters and needed less food than the huge dinosaurs. Many lived underground, in water, or in the air.

A group of small, birdlike flying dinosaurs also survived! They were the ancient relatives of living birds.

VEGAVIS

Vegavis was one of these survivors. This fish-eating bird was a relative of modern ducks and geese, and may have even honked like a goose! It was about the same size as a modern mallard duck.

QUIZ ANSWERS

Check your answers to the quiz questions HERE ...

PAGE 17:
QUICK QUIZ

- Deinonychus behaved like modern wolves.
- Hypsilophodon behaved like modern gazelles.
- Oviraptor behaved like modern penguins.
- Apatosaurus behaved like modern elephants.

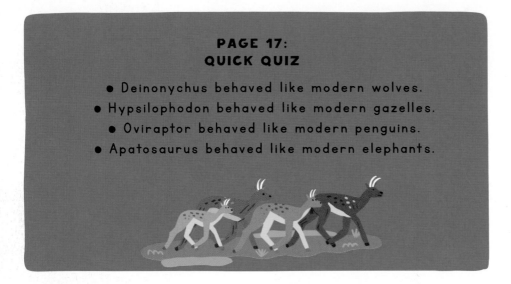

PAGE 23:
QUICK QUIZ

The bowls of food
belong to:

1. Protoceratops

2. Compsognathus

3. Fruitadens

4. Microraptor

PAGE 29:
QUICK QUIZ

T. rex had better
eyesight than
Carcharodontosaurus.
This is because forward-
facing eyes can both
focus on the same
object and provide a
better sense of how
near or far the object is.

PAGE 39:
QUICK QUIZ

It would take about
eight divers.